Josh

The Really Easy Brass Series
General Editor: John Ridgeon

The *Really* Easy Horn Book

Very first solos for horn in F with piano accompaniment

Christopher Gunning & Leslie Pearson

Faber Music Limited
London

Preface

You need only be able to play a few notes on the horn to make music. The 10 little pieces in this book have been written and selected with beginners in mind, but within the technical limitations this imposes there is plenty of scope for musical interest. The pieces are arranged progressively, so as well as musical satisfaction you can have the pleasure of hearing the step-by-step improvement in your playing. The piano accompaniments have been kept as simple as possible.

First Book of Horn Solos and *Second Book of Horn Solos* by Douglas Moore and Alan Richardson are also available.

Contents

1. Elegy

Christopher Gunning

28
35
p
42
mp
mp
49

56
mf
mf
63
70
77
p
mp

2. Valse Triste

Leslie Pearson

28
Ped.
35
42
49

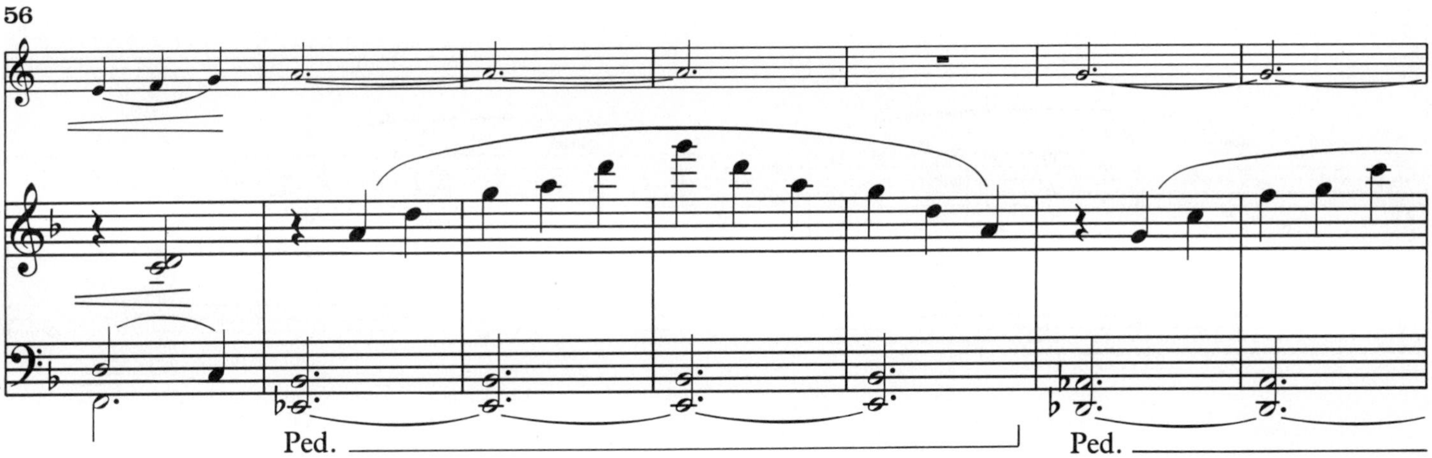

56

Ped.

Ped.

63

8ve

Ped.

3. Stepwise

Leslie Pearson

Moderato (♩ = 112)

mf

mf

6

11
16
21
26

32
37
42
poco allargando
48
rit.

4. Echoes

Christopher Gunning

18
rit.
Tempo I
mp
p
22
26
poco rit.
a tempo
poco meno mosso
mp
p sostenuto
30
poco
p

5. Largo Appassionato

Ludwig van Beethoven,
arr. Leslie Pearson

17
al Coda
p
22
mp
27
D.C. al segno e poi la Coda
poco rit.
f
32
CODA

6. Minuet

Johann Sebastian Bach,
arr. Leslie Pearson

7. Sad Café

Christopher Gunning

10
(solo)
mf
p
14
mp
18
rit.
a tempo
mf
p
mf
pp
22
poco rit.
meno mosso
p
8va

8. Girls and Boys

Leslie Pearson

32
8ve
dim.
pp
Ped.
39
mf
46
53

60
67
9. Rag Doll
Christopher Gunning
Allegretto (♩ = 84)
mp
sim.
f
5
1.

9
2.
f
(solo)
mf
14
p
mf
18
f
mf
p
23
fp
mp

28
mp
f
33
p
37
mf
f
mf
42
espress.
dolce
f sub.
Ped.
Ped.

10. Prelude Op.16 No.4

Alexander Skryabin,
arr. Christopher Gunning